FROM EMPLOYMENT
TO EMPOWERMENT

FROM EMPLOYMENT
TO EMPOWERMENT

**Attaining Financial Freedom and Personal
Empowerment During and After Paid Employment**

Ayo Emakhiomhe

authorHOUSE®

AuthorHouse™ UK Ltd.
1663 Liberty Drive
Bloomington, IN 47403 USA
www.authorhouse.co.uk
Phone: 0800.197.4150

Published by AuthorHouse   08/19/2013

ISBN: 978-1-4918-0288-5 (sc)
ISBN: 978-1-4918-0289-2 (e)

CONTENTS

ACKNOWLEDGEMENTS

If you have been my boss before, my colleague or worked with me in some way before while I was an employee, I thank you because, you are the characters in this drama, and I owe it to you.

I thank my father-Jehovah Efizzy for inspiration for this book and all the practical experiences shared in it, you indeed are the ultimate author of my life.

I also appreciate my pillar and better half for all her support and encouragement. I thank my family for giving me a life path that led to this book and now includes it.

My thanks go also to everyone not mentioned here but instrumental to this book before you today.

FOREWORD

Are you in any form of paid employment and wondering why you can't break free? Are you tired of working for money and want money to work for you? Have you been looking for the right path to take to move on to the next level in your job/career? Do you feel as an employee you are better than what you are getting presently? Do you have your life after paid employment adequately outlined and maybe even in motion? Do you seek financial freedom? Do you feel trapped on that job? Are you still happy with your job? Do you seek more happiness on the job? Do you feel you have lost your motivation to work?

If your response to any of the questions above was 'YES' then this book is a must read for you.

This is a look through the employee maze and a guide to assist the employee in attaining empowerment at all levels of their lives and live free to exit paid employment a success.

This book is for you if you are an employee in any industry. No matter how disperse the industries are, the principles of employee empowerment and financial freedom are the same and the issues affect us all as long as we are in paid employment; experience for the book I have learnt from my years of business development consultancy and paid employment. This experience I now want to share with you so that like me, you can live free.

Hop in lets go for the ride!

INTRODUCTION

We experienced how the global financial crisis affected those around us; friends, colleagues, subordinates, neighbors, superiors and retirees. No industry was spared especially those that were able or unable to cope with sudden job losses. As a live participant in the banking industry in Nigeria and a world observer of the financial crisis, I can accurately tell you that it has been a bitter pill to swallow, especially when you are not ready for it.

That is what inspired this book; to tell my colleagues and all those in paid employment that a day will surely come; it will be either voluntarily by retirement, resignation or forcefully by retrenchment or outright sack. What are you doing in preparation for that fateful day? It is never too early or too late, the time is now.

I was at a seminar sometime back where a former bank MD who is now into real estate was giving the story of how unprepared he was for life after banking and how he had struggled to stay overboard for a long time. He also talked about a former bank MD in one of the banks in Nigeria who retired in the early nineties and took his severance package in joy to go live the rest of his life in blissful glamour, after all, such a huge payoff will not finish for like another two life times, but to his amazement, it drained like a leaky pipe, as at the time he gave us this information, he is presently a door man at a bank in New York just to make ends meet. Why did this happen to him? He had the money and he worked for it, he probably also had plans to invest the money. And for a man of his vast financial experience, where did he go wrong?

My former landlord told me a story of a neighbor of mine in a previous neighborhood I stayed at Ojota, in Lagos Nigeria who worked and grew to the level of the chief accountant of his company, a multinational company in the breweries industry, when he resigned, he had a very good pay off, but as at today, he is just getting by. Is that how to retire into bliss?

A colleague of mine some time ago while I was still in paid employment was his branch head of operations, managing the assets and vault of the bank in a branch in Nigeria. After a while, he felt he was tired of the 'frustrating and oppressive system' (using his words) and that it was time to consolidate on his business he was working on part time and so he resigned. This was in mid 2012. As at November of 2012, I met him at an office where he came for a job interview and I asked him what went wrong. Why was he searching for a job so soon? He said business went sour and all his money went with it, so he is desperate to get some form of income, I probed further to find out where he missed it in the business and from our short interview it was obvious that he went into the business with focus on the purported income and never bothered mastering the business process and that got him fried. Why are we driven by money? Is it a means to an end or an end in itself?

We go to school in a system that indoctrinates us to read hard and get good grades so that when we get out we will get good jobs, no one teaches about preparing for retirement, true job satisfaction, money; we go out and reality fries us. A few veterans survive but never unscratched. I am sure it proves the saying that 'no story no glory', after all, these veterans are the celebrated self made millionaires and billionaires today. When we read their stories, will we say they were educated or empowered?

The other day, there was a slight delay in payment of salaries and I saw some people break down into tears; simply because they live from paycheck to paycheck. Is this the right way to live life? Especially in this era of financial meltdown, have we forgotten the stories of Enron or the Lehman brothers' saga so soon?[i]

One of the highest employers of labour in Nigeria is the banking sector; does that still hold today? It seems the trend is reversing due to economic down turn and technological advancements; will that your current job position be needed in your office in 3-5 years from now? What are you doing now about that?

This book is a wakeup call, a call to action, a call that there is another life beyond paid employment, a call that your life does not depend on that job, a call that you can do without your job, a call to a new life; a life of empowerment.

CHAPTER 1

LIFE AS AN EMPLOYEE

Paid employment can be fun. It is an excellent training ground for the business world. It provides immediate funding for your daily and life expenses. It gives you financial hope, gives you respect in your home and community, encourages you to plan into the future to achieve your dreams. But will that job always be there?

When do you plan on leaving that job? What do you plan to do when you leave?

More often than not, a lot of workers will readily churn out loads of plans and ideas as responses to the questions above. But the issue is how many of us have actually written them down as real plans with timelines and milestones?

The fact is that until you do this, you do not have a plan. So I ask again, what do you plan to do when you leave your job either voluntarily or otherwise?

A critical step to success in life is planning. There is a popular saying that 'he who plans to fail, fails to plan.' Strategy is all about planning and no wars are won without a successful strategy.

You should start planning and working towards your exit in any form it comes from your first day at work.

If you have not written a precise plan down on what you will be doing towards self actualization during your employment days and into retirement/resignation, finish this book and go start one immediately. If you have one written, then good for you, still finish this book and go perfect it. If it's perfected, have you been meeting your targets and timelines? If not, we still have an issue here. We will still talk more on planning later in this book.

If you need a guide to preparing a plan or a business plan, you can get it for free at www.coinboxng. com and download the free business plan guide. A more concise planning guide is at our blog page archive www. coinboxlimited.blogspot.com.

Paid employment is supposed to provide you with a platform for empowerment; first is self development, basic self actualization, and then serve as a platform to launch you into your dreams.

What I mean is that employment is same as your occupation, and your occupation is what you do to keep you occupied until the real deal comes through, your job is what you do in your occupation, your profession is what you profess (that is declare allegiance to) at a defined point in time. Remember that those you profess allegiance to are those who have significant influence over your life and achievements because what you say is what you become; so be sure of that profession you belong to and those in it and their primary tenets before you profess or have allegiance to them.

In all of the definitions above, the real deal is your work, your work is what defines you, it motivates you, it decides your level of satisfaction, it defines your habits and character, and your work should be your dream, your life plan, your life mission, your life goal. If you presently work where your job definition does not fall into this category then you are only occupied.

When occupied, here's what you think makes you happy or what makes you tick on that job;

THE SALARY MIRAGE.

For many employees, they feel that the solution to all their problems is either a fat salary or a fatter salary. The truth of the matter is that it is none of those, money is only a means to an end and not an end in itself, stop chasing joy and satisfaction in the wrong places, it's time to realign your priorities and your values.

For those of us looking for the highest paying jobs, stop it. Start looking for the most self fulfilling and satisfying job, the job that fits into your correct life definition, goals and value systems. I say this because in my country-Nigeria, a lot of people came into banking either out of definition of a fat salary will solve their problems or that it will solve all their money problems. Then they find out that the solution is not there and some now commit fraud or never reach optimal productivity on the job.

No matter your salary, Parkinson's Law which states that expenses will always grow to meet income, no matter the level of income, will always catch up with your salary.

If you are already stuck on your job, redefine and realign your reasons for working for your organisation and remove money from the equation. This will help you live longer and achieve more on the job and in your life. Life has to be defined properly to get the right success perspective. If you can't redefine your job then it's time to get another one.

When I graduated from University with my first degree, I went job hunting only to find out that as at that time in Nigeria, only two industries virtually existed with reasonable salaries to meet my perceived standards. That was the banking sector and the oil sector. A very large chunk of job seekers were chasing the jobs in the oil sector because the salaries paid there were very comfortable but the number of jobs available there was like ten (10%) percent or less than what existed in the banking sector. So I left the crowd and faced the banking sector to get myself a fat paying job.

I got the job within weeks and was started off with a comfortable salary although the economy then made the salary seem like peanuts and that was the first reality bite I got—the fat salary is not for new kids on the block like myself but for the experienced hands that had spent some time on the job. The new entry level employees that made the salary seem like heaven lived on credit and I learnt a long time ago that it was only the poor that had to take credit to meet the basic necessities of life. The rich took credit for investment and business expansion. I choose not to live a poor man's life.

> [I learnt a long time ago that it was only the poor that had to take credit to meet the basic necessities of life. The rich took credit for investment and business expansion. I choose not to live a poor man's life.]

After a while I realized that I was not happy on the job and seemed not to be making progress even though my salary had been increased twice in the last twelve months. I wanted promotion but was not getting it, I needed to work and be happy I was working but there was always this emptiness inside, dissatisfaction, discontent, pushing me further and further into the job, looking for more and more joy.

It was in this my quest that I realized that to succeed on the job you have to love the job like it was your own, work like you were the Managing Director and think that way too, whenever you needed to take a decision try and understand your company management to the point where you have a clear understanding of their thinking and their focus, what makes them tick. Knowing that, take every decision as 'if I were the boss what decision or line of action would I take on this issue? '

Once I started thinking and acting like this, I started getting noticed, I got commendations from the MD twice, I got my promotions and of course, I got more pay. But it was never enough and I wanted more every time.

POOR WORK AND LIFE BALANCE.

There was a day at the office that due to civil unrest we were asked to go home much earlier than usual, a colleague refused to leave, His reason 'I don't have anything to do at home', I was moved and this got me thinking 'how many other bankers are like him'. If at 10.00am you were asked to stop work and go home for the rest of the day, how many of you workers would get worried about going home?

A lot of bankers we ask this question get thrown off balance because their job is their life. But there is another life out there aside the job, many bankers in Nigeria do not have a social life any more, there is an imbalance. Some bankers have been alienated from their families because of their job schedules. They have been imbibed with the belief that it is how long you stay in the office that shows how hard you are working. At a time, I worked for some bankers that took it as a thing of pride of who stayed in the office the latest. I would like to know the banker in Nigeria who gets paid for working well beyond their official closing time on a daily basis. This is actually a lack of productivity and you are becoming more of a liability than an asset to that company.

I had a boss once, in one of our formal sessions, she actually confessed that having worked so long at the company, she would have resigned, but she can't because she had nothing else to do and nothing else planned. Her job had been her life, no friends, no family, no plans. After a while, she started to become a nuisance till she was forced out of the job. What a way to end a sterling career. Is that a balanced life?

When was the last time you read your employment letter? You are supposed to work for about 8 hours with a short break in-between. But some of us bankers do 12-16 hours daily but forget that there is no overtime pay; it is a herculean task enforcing labour laws in Nigeria where the work culture is still no different from the slave era due to the majority of minds still held by the poverty mentality of both the employer and the employee.

And this does not guarantee that the company will not do away with you once the need arises. Also, we give up our lunch break too thereby giving our life away for the same salary(sometimes less) and not a dime extra, sometimes no form of appreciation, just more complaints from our superiors/employers of how unduly we do our job and how uncommitted we are. We lose our family, friends, spouses and then, we lose the job. So was all the sacrifice worth it?

Everything in life is about creating balance, even God in the Bible demonstrated this when He created boundaries for the land and sea, the sky and the land, and rested on

7

the seventh day after creating the world in six days—He set up the law of balance with these acts. We need to set boundaries for everything and create time to rest and recreate outside work.

No matter how busy you are create time for family, friends, hobbies, fun outside work, self development, etc.

If you don't create this balance now, it's a natural law so you will have to pay for it later by which time it will be a very bitter pill and maybe even too late as there will be no one to socialize with then. And loneliness from the middle age leads to all kinds of sicknesses and early death. Lack of self development also leads to early grave because the day you stop growing is the day you start dying. Every time you do something to develop yourself; read a book, learn a language, learn a trade, learn an art, explore, discover, etc. you are growing.

AN ILLUSION OF INDISPENSABILITY.

Many employees' believe they are indispensable in their offices, they say things like "I am doing so well that my organisation cannot do without me." I am sorry to tell you this, but no one is indispensable. If you were indispensable then the organisation would shut down if suddenly you fall ill, or drop dead. At least, when you drop dead you get a moment of silence, but after that, someone has taken over your seat and (sorry to say this) the job goes on, probably even better than how it was run before.

Most organisations try to create balance such that no matter the volume of productivity/income an employee brings into an organisation, it should at no time be more than ten to twenty percent of the total productivity/income of such an organisation. Note that I am not saying that some companies will deliberately reduce your productivity, what I am saying is that the more you produce, the more valuable you will be to the organisation, but the onus is on management to distribute or support your inflow in such a way that if any unforeseen situation like the sudden resignation of such productive staff should occur, not more than 10% to 20% of business is lost which can be quickly recovered.

[The only organisation where you are indispensable is yours.]

And if the above analysis is true, then the only organisation where you are indispensable is yours.

A very proactive organisation will notice its highly productive staff and let them know how important they are to that organisation and will work hard at ensuring that such an employee is not lost and will go further to ensure that if such happens, there will be fallback systems.

A DECEPTIVELY PERFECT WORKING ENVIRONMENT

What holds in a standard work environment should hold in a standard economy. But in Nigeria only businesses and individuals that can afford to pay the high price that can get an environment where all the basic necessities exist; you get to work and there is power, the dispenser has water, intercom works, the system is on auto-cruise. What happens when you leave the system to a real Nigerian life scenario?

Nigeria as a country has a system that quickly assists you to realize this once you are out of the office.

But note that the standard life environment is slowly improving in Nigeria and a non-standard environment where you have to provide all your basic necessities/ infrastructures like roads, electricity, security, health, etc is becoming a thing of the past.

As an employee, working a long time in such an environment where trust is core gets into you and after a while, you assume everyone is like that. Wake up and smell the coffee dear, out there in the real world, not everyone is honest, and some who even try just can't be so. If everyone was as honest as you, we would not require law courts. In the real world, being street smart keeps you above board.

People actually go out there to look for gullible trusting workers like you and scam their money off them. They usually use that statement that it is a smooth system, just drop your money and get the returns.

Let's learn to do our homework and understand every system before we agree to go into it.

Things have been perfect in your work place (even your customers) does not mean that it's a perfect system out there.

TRUST

One of the cruxes of banking is TRUST. A banker must be trustworthy and full of integrity. The average banker has the tendency to trust all those around them too, probably because of the relatively high trust (integrity) level in their work environment. Stories abound about how ex-bankers have lost their severance packages and life savings to tricksters. To survive life outside employment, you have to be more cautious with people.

Do not go running a business or a deal with that person you know next to nothing about. Even an old friend you have not been in contact with for the last six months is not good enough to trust. As a money dealer (banker) for example, everyone wants a bite of that money you do not have and they will show all forms of pretense just to have it.

Also, as a rule, never go into a business you know next to nothing about. Ensure you have at least a basic idea of that business before you put your precious time and your hard earned money into it. If you go into such a venture, you have already thrown open enough opportunities to be cheated and to fail in that business. Never live by the illusion that your relative or your best friend will not or cannot cheat you; I am sorry to tell you that when it comes to money, this is very possible and it is better to prevent such than to allow such happen in the first place and start regretting later.

> [Do not go running a business or a deal with that person you know next to nothing about]

PAST EXPERIENCES.

A lot of us hold on to past experiences of either ourselves or those around us and use that as a reason to even probably not do anything about our future. Past experiences are supposed to be practical guides in the journey of life; they are books we learn from. Falling from a horse means getting back on it to be a better rider.

Have you ever considered what you did wrong or what the person whose bad experience you know of did not do correctly to have suffered the bad fate that came upon that person? This is what we should look for in such experiences so that we learn and not make that same mistake. After all, experience they say is the best teacher and you cannot buy experience.

A while back, one of my first ventures was a telecoms business where we offered telephone calls at a premium and sold phones and recharge cards.

This business recouped its capital within 3 months, and things were going well. In six months we had two offices with staff working, by the seventh month my relative who was my partner sold out the business and disappeared from existence. I searched without success for this relative till I gave up on the search. I felt like dying then because I had put all my life savings into this deal. But what did I do after; I sat down and thought of where I went wrong. After careful analysis and deliberations with others who were successful in this line of business, we found my faults and how to prevent such from happening again next time, also, we had no written agreement but worked on trust, I actually had no control over the business, we were working on 'an understanding'. There was no structure on ground, nothing to use to hold anyone accountable.

Today, I have been able to set up other businesses that are doing well, structures are on ground and there is a functional system for every sphere of the businesses. Why is this so? I learned from my mistakes and used that to improve on my next enterprise. I took the money lost as the cost of practical lessons in business class.

PENSION/GRATUITY.

A lot of us are deceived by the belief that our pension and gratuity will take care of us. What we do not realize is that when we get to that stage, our standard of living will have been much higher and the kind of money we will get as pension will definitely not be able to sustain us and more often than not, when the stark reality hits us in the face, most pensioners now get frustrated to the point of death in regret. This is an opportunity for you not to suffer that fate. Do you have a plan for your gratuity? If you wait till you get the money before you plan for it, the money will not be there when you need it.

Why is your pension/gratuity your only source of income at old age? You should create multiple streams of income for yourself. Your current salary and job should be a means to an end, not an end in itself, save and invest a lot of your current earnings. If your pension is all you have, it will soon dry up. Even the bible says that a good man leaves an inheritance for his children and his children's children[ii]. What inheritance are you planning on leaving for your future generations be they born or unborn?

The best pension you can leave for yourself is a business that will take care of you at your current standards long after you have retired and even your generations to come.

SAVINGS.

Savings is very good, but note that no matter the sum you save, the returns on savings is always lower than the current inflation rate annually and in some cases, the bank charges on your account is more than the savings interest paid you. What this means is that if a bank pays you about 2% interest on your savings annually and the inflation rate is 5% annually, that means that your money in the bank is reducing in value by 3% every year, which means that the real value of your money will be less than 30% what it is meant to be in ten years time. More practically, if you were saving one hundred thousand naira yearly at 2% interest annually and your country's inflation rate was 5% annually, that means that after 10 years your investment will be as the table below in real terms

Year	Savings value at 2% annual interest rate	Savings value at 5% annual inflation rate
0	100,000.00	—
1	102,000.00	97,000.00
2	104,040.00	98,940.00
3	106,120.80	100,918.80
4	108,243.22	102,937.18

5	110,408.08	104,995.92
6	112,616.24	107,095.84
7	114,868.57	109,237.75
8	117,165.94	111,422.51
9	119,509.26	113,650.96
10	121,899.44	115,923.98

This means that you would have lost over seventy (70%) of the amount of money you would have made if you invested in a platform that gave you a minimum returns above the average inflation rate.

Cash savings should be considered for short term basis and not for long term returns.

You should always save for the basic economic reasons like paying your bills, emergencies and for defined investment vehicles/platforms.

For emergencies, you should always have some form of cash savings available to withstand the shock like sudden job loss, accidents, etc. but always look for investments of medium and long term basis to move your cash to because under normal circumstances the least paying investment is your cash savings.

Your personal savings should be in easily convertible instruments like Treasury bills, Bonds, Stocks, commercial

[Your personal savings should be in easily convertible instruments like Treasury bills, Bonds, Stocks, commercial papers, and many other similar short to medium term investment instruments.]

papers, and many other similar short to medium term investment instruments. And it should not be more than twenty to thirty percent of your gross annual income. That means that if you earn NGN100, 000 gross incomes annually, you should advisably not keep more that NGN30, 000 in cash or cash convertible short to medium term convertible investment instruments.

Also once you have a comfortable sum of cash somewhere, there will always suddenly appear a need to push the cash to which is usually more of an expense rather than an investment. It is when you have cash stacked up in savings that you suddenly realize that you don't have enough clothes in your wardrobe or your house is too small for your status. Or a colleague suddenly has an urgent need to borrow half of that money for a family emergency of which you might not get that money back thereafter or get it in such piecemeal that it makes nonsense of the money.

Warren Buffet, one of the world's richest men has had his wealth growing astronomically in the last twenty years, but he has been staying in the same house for all that period. Let's learn from successful people like him.

CHAPTER 2

HAVING A LIFE IN PAID EMPLOYMENT

If you agree with me to any extent on all we have discussed so far, then we need to move to the next level in your life which is wholesomeness, this can only be achieved by living a well rounded and realistic life, a life of empowerment during and after the job.

Being empowered means putting your job in the right perspective, setting your priorities right and acting on the big picture which is your life and not just your job.

Being empowered makes you larger than life and places you above your current job situation, be it positive or otherwise. When you are underwater, you are struggling to survive; that's a situation where you will grab even a twig and any other thing around you to stay alive. When you are empowered you are above board, when you are above board, your worry is not survival, you are relaxed, and you look and see ahead, you plan, you strategize, and you succeed.

The following should assist in achieving this.

BALANCE:

Ensure you maintain a good work and life balance while in paid employment. It is excellent to enjoy your work. However, your job should not be the sole source of your happiness. Learn to enjoy living, to enjoy relationships, family, get hobbies, etc. plan to close early from the time you resume duty in the morning, prepare a daily schedule of activities to guide you through, learn to categorize your activities between urgent and important and not urgent and not important. Use office hours for office work. By doing this, you will be able to finish your day's work on time and face your life after work. Live your life after work in a balanced trend between rests, family, self development, your personal business, socialization, God and planning.

REST:

Ensure you go on all your annual vacations and every other breaks in-between, not once or half in three years and spend the leave period to reflect on your life. It's a golden opportunity to see the other side of life and to prepare you for life after paid employment.

What you need understand is that work does not end, but your life ends, time off work on vacation doing things outside your normal work routine or just relaxing helps prolong your life. Note that you cannot achieve this without planning for it. Always take a pen and plan your vacation year in advance (this includes the finance for it). Also, it is not only when a vacation is expensive that it is worth taking, it is worth taking when it is planned to be fun and relaxing.

There are so many pocket friendly vacation plans both locally and abroad. It's even part of relaxation to plan this.

> [What you need understand is that work does not end, but your life ends, time off work on vacation doing things outside your normal work routine or just relaxing helps prolong your life.]

SECURITY SAVINGS:

You should have liquid savings up to the equivalent of at least 3-6 months of your monthly net pay set aside for the unexpected events or simply kept as a Security Saving, which you could fall back on if you have to leave your job suddenly. Experiences have shown that the first 3-6 months are very crucial for someone that loses his job suddenly. Your security savings will stabilize you and enable you to think straight about what to do next. Note that this amount need not be cash in a savings account; it can be fixed deposit, bonds, treasury bills, commercial papers, or even shares, as long as it is easily convertible to cash.

This sounds similar to savings I mentioned earlier, but I had to put this separately for emphasis.

SUPPORT YOUR SPOUSE.

Encourage your spouse to engage in an income-generating activity if he/she is not already doing so, however small the activity. Reason is that when the dry times come, he/she would be able to understand first of all and then support at such times. But if he/she is not financially engaged previously, he/she would find it hard to understand that there can be a time of no money, your spouse might think that it's probably those times again when you just do not want to release money.

Please understand that it is good especially for the women folk to not get overly engaged combining work and home. If you feel your wife should not work, fine. But note that we are in a capitalist system where the middle class that has once disappeared has started to re-emerge and evolve and to meet with the demands on the pockets [as long as you are an employee and not an employer, you remain in the middle class of society and no matter you income, you will only live as a HNE—High net worth Employee and not as an Upper class individual who are HNI's—High Net worth Individuals.] of the average middle class family like the average bank employees of all levels, it is usually increasingly necessary for the two spouses to work. The job does not have to be a 9 to 5 job. It can be a network marketing venture or an NGO[iii] (voluntary work) for which he/she dictates the pace and time of service.

Note also that as long as you are an employee and not an employer, you remain in the middle class of society and no matter you income, you will only live as a HNE—High net worth Employee and not as an Upper class individual who are HNI's—High Net worth Individuals.

WATCH YOUR COSTS.

Always spend less than you earn (always resist the temptation to live above your means), separate necessity from luxury. For example you need a good shirt, but you don't need a shirt worth half your salary. Then invest what is left in money markets, stock markets, property markets, enterprises, etc. use a good portion of your current salary to build multiple streams of income that will sustain you when you cannot work again/in retirement.

What you should understand is that a lot of these people that buy big cars and wear expensive clothes don't do that with their salary, they do that with returns on investment. Do you have an investment that can buy you that multi-million naira car? If no, why are you interested in buying that—set your priorities right.

A minimum of 25% of your income should go to savings/ investments, others can be shared as 30% rent, 10% domestic, 10% on self development and on like that (don't forget God's 10% in your sharing formula).

FALL-BACK PLAN.

What is your back-up plan? That is, set out a written plan on paper or on your personal computer/tablet computer what you will be engaged in within the first 6 months in the eventuality of a sudden job loss/resignation. Ensure the plan is flexible enough for periodic reviews. Or you can simply set up an endowment or permanent disability cover for yourself and family. Have you set up that education trust or even that trust fund for your child/spouse/family?

I was at one time of the opinion that saving was difficult not to mention an endowment until I came across some colleagues of mine whose salary I can afford to pay. But at that time they had set up part time businesses from which they had made enough returns to support their family and build their own house with. So with my fat salary, I don't have a dime in savings, but here is someone whom I earn a salary that is more than ten times over his own who is not just a business owner but also a landlord. I felt ashamed of myself. But that got me thinking and acting, that was my leverage.

Also, prepare a plan of action with specific timelines and milestones as to when you plan to resign from that job. What you need so much to understand is that your salary (no matter how high it seems to be) should not be an end in itself. It should be a means to an end; that end you should have in mind is financial independence. As long as you collect and rely on a salary, you are a financial slave still

[As long as you collect and rely on a salary, you are a financial slave still fighting for financial independence.]

22

fighting for financial independence. Can you take yourself to that promise land of financial independence? It is up to you and you alone.

Prepare your plan in black and white written down like a specific business proposal; like a treasure map to lead you to your hidden treasure and surely it will. Stop idealizing, start putting it on paper, stop procrastinating, and start implementing your plan immediately.

SELF DEVELOPMENT.

A lot of workers are very guilty of this, and it is still being considered who to blame for this, whether to blame the system or the workers themselves. I remember a day in a particular bank I worked with sometime back. I was to take my annual leave and use part of it to sit for my professional examinations. My then zonal head turned it

[We have to take the bull by the horns and do the needful; a job can be taken from us at any point in time, but our education and experience can never be taken from us.]

down. Her reason was that 'your basic qualification is all you need to progress in the Nigerian banking industry and nothing more', so if that was why I was going on leave she will have to decline, I had to change the reason for my leave to 'personal reasons' to get my leave granted. But the truth is that this is what the Nigerian banking system seems to practice and believe in today. But I was not distracted by

23

her speech that day because it was part of my contingency plan and I am better for it today.

But this is not restricted to our banks in Nigeria alone; a lot of companies are guilty of this in so many sectors and industries. We have to take the bull by the horns and do the needful; a job can be taken from us at any point in time, but our education and experience can never be taken from us.

How many books do you read in a month, how many seminars do you attend? Are you still waiting in line for your company to send you on that training you can actually afford to pay for by yourself? What kind of books do you read? Do you read only those soft sell magazines? What kind of CD's/DVD's do you listen to? Do you watch only entertainment or movies on Cable TV like watching only E channel or Africa Magic on DSTV? Or are you the football hero who watches more football than the players who play the game? How many porn sites and gossip pages do you visit online daily and how long do you spend on these sites? Have you ever considered converting this time to money to see how much you have been losing yearly?

We have to play down on all these, read more books that will help with your leadership development, books that will sharpen your technical skill in an area of business or investment, read material that will improve your level of financial literacy, read books that will improve on your relational, social and networking abilities, watch both local and international news and consider how they affect you and your economy and what opportunities you can seize from such information. Read less of those end time series, add studies in business, history, management, finance, economy, politics, discoveries (authenticated not presumed), read on dressmaking, network marketing, strategy, baking, marketing, managing excellent relationships and personality development, public speaking, communication, poise, negotiation, job improvement skills; **READ! READ! READ!!**

Listen to CD's/ DVD's attend seminars and trainings at least once a quarter. Subscribe to and read business magazines and journals. Sales men (even Bank marketers) Learn from your clients and work at understanding their business dynamics much better, be an expert or even a consultant on their business, (it is not just about cheque collection.) A good businessman will want to do business with a person who is genuinely interested in their business, and they would even do more business with a marketer/ sales man who is an expert in their line of trade and be sure of plenty of unsolicited referrals when you have been tested and proven. The relationship between a businessman and his banker should be like a doctor to a patient, if the patient considers you competent and can consult you not just on when next you can come to collect the next cheque, but on his/her business issues, on new developments in his/ her business and how it affects that specific organisation, on ways of making your customers' business better, you will become an essential part of that organisation and it's only natural for you to have all the organisations business. As you become good at this, you have laid down a solid foundation and training for your business tomorrow.

INTEGRITY

Be known for keeping your word. Live a lifestyle of integrity. Make transparency, honesty, and high integrity your watchwords. Your social network (local associations, town meeting, office, church, mosque, club, etc.) play highly essential roles in stabilizing you in the short & long term before and after leaving paid employment. However, hardly will your former acquaintances want to associate with you, post-work, if your integrity and honesty were in doubt while still employed.

A lot of referrals and businesses I got immediately after paid employment were from old colleagues and customers while in paid employment.

A word that came from all the referrals was always that I was recommended as trustworthy with integrity and that means that in running a business, customers pay you also because of the value of your integrity and not just for your good/service no matter the quality.

NETWORKING

Enlarge your social capital, network, network and network. Work on and grow your network. The network you develop now will support you at initial exit from your job or at the kick off of your business. What association are you a member of, what society are you a part of, what value are they adding to you or your future, keep the positive ones close to you by participating in their activities as often as possible. These groups will form your initial base when you exit. 'My job is very demanding, I don't have time to socialize/interact' is a lie conjured by you. It's all about priorities and perspectives.

Join investment clubs/groups, cooperative societies, NGO's or simply form your own.

When you join such groups, you do not only network, you get to learn business and investments styles that work, share experiences, see the perspectives of other sectors of the economy, see and experience reality.

Start a part-time business while employed. Look for an opportunity to fill. Look for what people in your environment need, and work towards meeting the needs at a fee or even volunteer your services and use that to learn and interact, it is a great way to humble yourself, learn and relax.

You could in fact create a need! For example, are you a chartered accountant? What stops you from 2-4 hours of consultancy at a fee on weekends? What happened to referral marketing or direct sales/network marketing?

DIET AND EXERCISE

It is so important to keep fit to live a healthy old life. It has been discovered that the more you exercise the more work you can do and you stay healthy longer.

Exercise helps in increasing the flow of oxygen and blood to your brain, this keeps your brain fresh and healthy and this in turn keeps you at top notch.

Consult your Doctor for the right exercise routine to keep you fit and ensures you exercise at least 10 to 30 minutes daily.

Good healthy food and its importance cannot be over emphasized. Please note that it is not the volume of food you eat but the quality of food that keeps you alive and well. Always ensure that you keep a very healthy combination of food each time you eat. Consult with your dietician on the best combination of food for you. Try as much as possible to avoid eating between meals, take extra efforts to eat more of fresh foods and less processed foods.

THE GOD FACTOR

The God factor is very essential and cannot be over-emphasized. Some years ago, a magazine did a research on the factors that were needed to make people millionaires. One thing they all agreed to was the God factor. They say there is that upper being that just upgrades them to succeed. Therefore even after having the best of plans and even while still on the job, have God in mind positively and you cannot fail.

Also, it was from the God factor and reading my bible that my mindset was changed dramatically when I discovered that my line of thought was not as it should be. I was in church one Sunday listening to a message from my pastor, he made a reference to a passage in the Bible that changed my entire mindset and I realized that this is how the average employee around here thinks even when the bible says otherwise. The passage was in the book of proverbs chapter 24 verse 27 (New King James Version): **Prepare your outside work,**

Make it fit for yourself in the field;

And afterward build your house.[iv]

Basically, what it says is that you should build your business before you build your house. That means to me that your business should build your house. And a business that can build a house will surely build many other houses. It changed my mindset because the thinking of a lot of us employees around here is to earn a good salary and build/buy your house and you are made. I am sorry to tell you that this is in the reverse. **BUILD YOUR BUSINESS.**

This point would have been arguable if we had an economy in Nigeria where the government did most of the house building or mortgage was readily available, but we know in Nigeria, this does not hold; you build your house, create/ lay your streets, build your own water supply system, and get your own security but you still have to pay your tax. God bless Nigeria.

KNOW YOURSELF

Do a SWOT analysis of yourself; check for your strengths, weaknesses, opportunities available to your kind of person to make optimal use of and issues, items, situations, etc. that might pose a threat to those identified opportunities.

This is called self discovery. This leads to self mastery. When you know what you are capable of, you can focus only on those

[When you know what you are capable of, you can focus only on those activities that illuminate from your strength and over time you will naturally be a super star at such activities]

activities that illuminate from your strength and over time you will naturally be a super star at such activities and it is not usual to be a super star and be broke. SWOT stands for Strengths, Weaknesses, Opportunities and Threats. When you know your strengths and weaknesses, you will know how to go about seizing the opportunities around you and opposing any threats that will arise from that.

TAKE LARGE DOSES OF PATIENCE AND PERSEVERANCE

A lot of us are used to those Cinderella business stories where a business starts and rakes in megabucks from day one. Well, just like Cinderella, it is a story. A business/investment is like a baby, you need time to nurture it, let it grow, be patient, learn to plow your profits back into it up to a certain level where it can feed itself.

Be patient, there will be ups and downs, learn to persevere in the down times. Focus on the end goal. Plan what you will do with your success. You cannot help but to succeed.

CHAPTER 3

WHEN YOU SUDDENLY LOSE YOUR JOB

It is difficult setting and implementing plans; it is more difficult facing a sudden change like losing a job. But how you react to this situation is key to the path your future will follow; do you react proactively being prepared or irrationally being unprepared?

Summarizing from the words of Stephen R. Covey in his book—THE 8TH HABIT^Y; the space between action and reaction is the real you. For example, this is where job loss is the action or stimulus and the reaction is the resultant effect you allow to occur.

Below are some tips to help you through this unforeseen circumstance when it occurs.

A. WATCH YOUR ATTITUDE;

On and off the job, your Attitude determines your altitude. Learn to put your attitude under control. If you're asked to go, it certainly won't be the end of life; but rather the beginning of another phase of your life. It is a challenge you must face with optimism and determination to succeed. Dejection, depression, pessimism, and fear are willing companions at this crucial stage of your life. Forcefully reject their companionship. Have a positive attitude and a positive outlook and everything positive will come to you. But if you take a negative attitude, you will get negative results.

[Dejection, depression, pessimism, and fear are willing companions at this crucial stage of your life. Forcefully reject their companionship.]

To dwell a bit on this, we need to understand that life is not about the position or money, life is about the person—YOU.

I will give you a practical example. If for example the state governor decides to pitch his office at your house, it will not stop the state business, what usually happens is that while he/she is there in your house, the state will provide all that is necessary to enable the governor to perform his functions to move the state forward. That is, your house is transformed to the state house because a person was there—the Governor, not simply because there was money to transform it. And that is how it is for all of us. You get transformed when you transform your mind and that affects your attitude. Have a positive mindset and you will have a positive attitude and you get transformed and attract only positive results. Always look at things from the brighter side.

Always be careful with the way you react to sudden job loss, it is always advisable you use the 90/10 principle as stated by Stephen R. Covey[vi]. It states that 10% of life is decided by what happens to you and 90% of life is decided by how you react. If you react positively with a good attitude you will have a bright future but if otherwise, the outcome is easily predictable.

B. IT'S NOT YOUR FAULT

Self confidence is important. Don't blame yourself or anybody or any institution for that matter. Instead, focus all your energy on what you want to do next. Focus it on that contingency plan you had set out earlier. The mind is a very (if not the most powerful tool) powerful tool for success. It is so powerful that if you focus on anything long enough, even if it is not available or existent, it will show up on your behalf.

Before you lost that job you spent only 1-3 hours daily on that your contingency plan and there were surely some results, now you have 24 hours to do this, you cannot but succeed.

C. DON'T ASK FOR ALMS, ASK FOR ARMS

Do not give up and go begging; otherwise your friends and family will start avoiding you. Rather, get to friends to discuss your business ideas and seek their sincere opinion and support (and even collaboration).

[Do not give up and go begging; otherwise your friends and family will start avoiding you. Rather, get to friends to discuss your business ideas and seek their sincere opinion and support (and even collaboration).]

I wish to mention here that more often than not, we have great business ideas and plans and a challenge we face is capital. Well, I think I have noticed over a long period that the issue is not capital, the issue is packaging. A well packaged business plan that addresses the key issues like structure, cash flow, systems, etc will attract the needed capital, sometimes it might take a while, but it will come. Also, a lot of us like to do it alone. No one is a lone ranger, no man is an island unto himself and even God realized that man should not be alone[vii].

Take advantage of the power of synergy. Money goes after value; does your business plan show/have value? If passed through fire, will it come out like fine gold? *You can get guide to writing a business plan free at www.coinboxng. com (free PDF version) or www.coinboxlimited.blogspot.com.*

If your contingency plan can pass the value test, people will even pay just to look at it.

Check out the success stories—Microsoft, Apple, OANDO, Zenith bank, Berkshire Hathaway, Forbes; Success was never achieved alone.

D. WHAT HAPPENED TO YOUR BACK UP PLAN?

Decide quickly what you want to do, don't just sit down brooding; will it be to:

- ✓ Get another job. You must ensure that you have trained yourself well on that your job to have acquired skills that make you invaluable in your job delivery.
- ✓ Or start a business. This is the season for entrepreneurship, ride the tides and subdue the waves; with your contingency plan you have what it takes to win.

Remember you had written a plan down, go implement it.

E. REDUCE YOUR DAILY EXPENSES

Minimize your daily expenses as you live on your security savings. If you are married, confide in your spouse and kids, and together you should work out what to do next, and how to live on your Security Savings so it takes you far enough.

Cut off those expenses like unnecessary chit chat on the phone, impulsive drives to a 'friends' place that will not in any way help with your business plan or your job search. This is not the time to buy new clothes. It is not a must to buy that uniform like attire we call "Aso ebi" in Nigeria, you are not an outcast for not buying it; you are wise. Reason is that after that celebration, that couple/person will not die; the person will be around to do many more celebrations for which your financial stand will be good enough to even foot that bill.

Separate luxuries from necessities. This is only temporal pending when you find your feet.

Also, make sure that if you are married you communicate and plan all this effectively with your spouse and kids. I will expect you to do this too with your to be spouse if that is your current status. Else get a mentor to relate this with and a close friend/confidant who shares your vision.

F. READY, FIRE, AIM

Plan what to do with your severance package. Never rush into any business venture you are not familiar with. Carefully consider any business/investment idea anybody might bring your way. Talk with business development consultants like myself before you proceed. Talk to investment advisors and financial experts. Make your personal research into the venture before you jump in. Do not let others do your home work for you.

Ensure structures exist that will offer some form of security/ insurance or serve as red lights that things are not according to plan before going into that deal.

G. RELAX

Learn to relax. Never put yourself under pressure to achieve. You don't have to prove anything to anyone. Be realistic in your planning and plan and act prayerfully. Be patient with yourself and others.

Whenever a sudden job loss occurs, it is usually advisable not to act immediately, take time out to relax and sit back and analyze and assess the situation. If possible take a break of 4 to 6 weeks to clear your head and be able to chart a more focused path forward. A job loss is not the end of the road it is only a fail forward as John C. Maxwell would say[viii] or simply consider it as a sharp bend on the road of life.

Once you are relaxed you will be able to see clearly and take focused, objective and unbiased decisions concerning your future and be able to separate good advice from adulterated ones.

Uche an old colleague of mine was a very dedicated hard working employee. She gave virtually her all to the organisation where she worked more often to the detriment of her family and social relationships. With the financial banking reforms of 2008 in Nigeria, she was actually among the first to be let go as a redundant staff.

Initially, it was a shocker for her, but with support and comfort from her husband, she decided to relax and truly define herself. It was in this process she realized that she had not been devoting any proper time to her family but to her job and that her job had not actually been as fulfilling as she had been able to convince herself. Initially, she hated her boss with a passion on the basis that she said it was her boss that must have submitted her name as the one to be let go in the department and never hid this from any one.

She started a small sea food supply business which she had been running haphazardly while working and within a short while, she got so happy with the business and more fulfilled such that it can be seen all over her with the way she glowed every time we saw her. I asked her for the secret to the change and she said she thought that the banking environment was perfect for her but now she realized she has more satisfaction having control over her time and income and being able to face her relationships more seriously.

She actually now sent a text message to her former boss, thanking her for putting her name on the redundancy list as it has been a wonderful and life changing experience for her. She also stated that she has never for one day missed working in the bank and will not return for any reason.

H. MENTOR

Get a mentor for your perceived line of business and for your career.

A relationship between a mentor and a mentee is defined as mentoring. It is the process for which a more knowledgeable and experienced person (the mentor) in a particular business, profession guides a less experienced and knowledgeable person (the mentee) through the ranks.

It can be formal or informal, face-to-face or through other means, what is important is the dissemination of information and constant regular contact over a period of time. It is about an ongoing relationship of learning, dialogue and challenge[ix].

A mentor is very important because your mentor helps greatly minimize your errors, speeds up your progress and holds you accountable.

A mentor need not be the perfect human being, but the reasonable person you can respect and who is far more knowledgeable than you in that venture. It can also be your customer or consultant. It can be more than one person and you are usually required to have your contingency plan ready before you meet your mentor.

CHAPTER 4

MOVING INTO EMPOWERMENT

Empowerment involves Visioning, self definition, planning and implementation, effective life management, leadership and Legacy.

If you are not empowered, you will not be able to appreciate fully or act well on all what has been discussed so far.

According to Wikipedia—Empowerment also includes encouraging and developing the skills for self sufficiency, with the focus on eliminating the future need for charity or welfare in the individuals or the group.[x]

If you are self sufficient, you will not need any group, individual or governments support to survive. That means you will not need your pension or children support to go on that annual vacation, change your car, and so many other things you can think of.

Empowerment is teaching you to fish rather than giving you fish to eat.

If you are empowered, you will be more of a great asset to your organisation than a liability. You will be more of an asset to yourself than a liability. When you are empowered, you become proactive in all areas of your life, you are focused and goal oriented, you become better, no matter how good you already are.

The crux of this book is on this word—EMPOWERMENT. From the preceding chapters to the chapters thereafter, I want you empowered, to be able to live a life of success, balance, satisfaction and financial freedom while on the job and thereafter.

To be empowered you have to take the following steps

- ✓ Define yourself
- ✓ Plan
- ✓ Effective life management
- ✓ Lead

SELF DEFINITION

The best way to fulfill your potential is by being yourself. You will not achieve great results by being someone else. When you copy others, the best you will ever be is a photocopy, we are all unique and it is this uniqueness that defines and leads to our greatness and self fulfillment in life.

Another definition of your uniqueness is your USP-Unique Selling Point; what is that thing about you that no other person has. Is it about the way you think, act, and respond/ react, what you see, your emotions, your aura, look for it! When you find your USP, you have found a major weapon in your arsenal for empowerment and success.

It is time to discover our USP-our strength. We would be guided by Simon Phillips[xi] in achieving this:

Think through the things that make you unique, those things that make up your strengths, those things you do exceptionally well. Write them down and list them in order of priority. The number 1 item is your strongest and it is the one item that people will immediately use to recognize you.

Having discovered that, now go out daily and find every opportunity to demonstrate this unique quality. As you hit the road daily, note the following:

- ✓ We identify too closely with what we do instead of who we are.
- ✓ You are a person, not a job title.

- ✓ Your occupation is what occupies your time not what you invest your time on.
- ✓ You are not defined by what you do but by who you are.
- ✓ You are everything, and, everything is you.
- ✓ Maximize the value that you get from every moment that you live
- ✓ Activity is the key and is only the reason why successful people benefit from momentum in their lives and in their businesses
- ✓ Learn to take risks. The risk of riskless living is the greatest risk of all.—Stephen Covey
- ✓ FEAR—this is False Evidences Appearing Real; it has no power in your life, stop giving your time to it.
- ✓ Never point a finger of blame at someone else, throw solutions at others instead. Successful people do not dwell on issues that are not contributing to their goals. Before you pass the buck, lay the blame or find the fault, look at the 4 fingers pointing back at you.
- ✓ Think positive always.

To define yourself, you have to define your personal mission/vision and state what you will want your life to be defined as representing when you die. Have a personal mission statement. Define your values; state those ones you will never bend or give-in for anything else. Please put these in writing and place it where you can see it often.

What would you want as your epitaph when you die? Think on this and state it, then reverse from there to this present time and start living your life focusing on those things that would help you in achieving this goal.

Break this goal and every other goal in your life to little pieces, set milestones and timelines to measure achievement along this line of action.

Also set up reward systems for you to celebrate whenever each milestone is reached. Note that your milestone should be realistic.

The reward need not be something humongous, maybe a day off your usual routine, dinner out, chocolate, that shirt you have been craving, a coffee break, anything

[When you learn to celebrate small victories, the big victories will show up to be celebrated.]

nice and simply at your discretion. When you learn to celebrate small victories, the big victories will show up to be celebrated.

Next make a list of the five most important things and the five most important people in your life. Do they represent the person (you) that was just defined above? If yes, spend more time on these, if not, commit today to making these people and things a priority in your life.

Taking some guide from Simon Phillips[xii], let us consider how often we take time out to reflect on our lives: what are we contributing, how do we benefit those around us, who we have become.

To discover who you really are, for the next 1 or 2 weeks, move around more consciously and note the following (possibly take some notes)

- ✓ Listen to how people talk to you; people talk to you with intonations and inflections about how they feel about you

- ✓ Listen to how you talk to others; a passage from the bible states that 'A good man out of the good treasure of his heart brings forth good; and an evil man out of the evil treasure of his heart brings forth evil. For out of the abundance of the heart his mouth speaks'[xiii]. Your words say a lot about who you are; it tells us where you are going to and where you are coming from.

- ✓ Reflect on the number of times you get annoyed or frustrated. When you know where you are going to your patience will be natural, when you are full of love, you anger will be rare, when you are wise, your frustration will be a needle in a haystack.

- ✓ Check how many times you smile; learn to appreciate everything about life genuinely, you live life only once.

- ✓ Monitor how many times you say 'thank you' genuinely; learn to be truly grateful for everything, no one owes you anything, you owe yourself and your world everything. Celebrate small victories.

- ✓ Check how often you plan, implement and review your actions. He, who fails to plan, plans to fail.

- ✓ Reflect on how many new friends you have made; life is about relationships, seek them, treasure them, everyday. Make it a point to make at least 1 new friend a month for life, move out of that comfort zone, RELATE!

- ✓ Ask yourself what you want people to do for you, then grab the initiative and do it for *them*[xiv].

Next, you appraise yourself

- ✓ Do a SWOT analysis (analysis of Strengths', Weaknesses, Opportunities and Threats) of yourself.
- ✓ What is your personality type? Are you a Melancholy, Sanguine, Phlegmatic or a Choleric? You can get lots of guides on this online with lots of free tests, reports, analysis and advice.
- ✓ What is your peak production time of the day? Do you work better in the morning, Afternoon, Evening or night? Put the activities that require your peak in your most productive time of the day.

Once you do a complete self appraisal, you can now leverage on those activities, events and people that expound your strengths and help improve on your weaknesses.

LEADERSHIP

In building construction, the foundation of a building is what decides on the size of the building. A very shallow foundation will produce a very shallow and small building. A deep, strong foundation will give rise to a very tall and awesome building.

This same principle in building construction can be likened to leadership; the depth of your leadership foundation decides the depth of leadership you offer.

A management theory has it that an organisation can never be bigger than the leader. That means that the bigger the organisation, the bigger the leader literally. This is not about the physical attributes of the leader, but the leadership depth of the person at the helm of affairs.

In building construction, we know that it's the combination of technology and building materials that decides the strength of the foundation; what then defines the strength of the foundation of a leader?

The leadership depth of a person is the embodiment and content of the person of a leader—the mind and spirit behind the leader.

What is the content of the mind of the leader? What is his/her focus? What motives drives his/her actions? What level of spiritual balance do you have as a leader?

[The leadership depth of a person is the embodiment and content of the person of a leader—the mind and spirit behind the leader.]

What is your personal mission/vision? These are questions that scream for answers.

Your mission is a cause(s) you want to achieve in life and your vision is how you go about achieving your mission. Examples of missions are eradication of poverty, cure to cancer, being number one in the provision of fast food services, the world's best in products distribution and logistics, and so much more. Your mission is usually constant over time while your vision changes with progress and realities.

For this discourse, I will hone in on two (2) foundational pillars; these are focus and self discipline. These two provide the foundation for solid leadership. Focus is doing one thing at a time, concentrating all your energy and resources at ensuring the success of a venture, project or activity, be it as simple as reading a book or as complex as completing a project. This should be applied in every area of your life, from your job to your relationships and life goals. Self discipline is doing the right things at the right time even when you don't feel like it and you have no one to encourage you to do it. It takes self discipline to go through a personal weight loss program and succeed. Self discipline is working when you are meant to be working even if the boss is not around to ensure you do that. Self discipline is the best antidote for procrastination.

[Focus is doing one thing at a time, concentrating all your energy and resources at ensuring the success of a venture, project or activity, be it as simple as reading a book or as complex as completing a project. This should be applied in every area of your life, from your job to your relationships and life goals. Self discipline is doing the right things at the right time even when you don't feel like it and you have no one to encourage you to do it.]

To gain and sustain focus and self discipline we must carry out the following as stated by John C. Maxwell in his 'Maxwell Leadership Bible'[xv]

1. Develop and guard your mind: your entire life should be like a sieve, allowing only what is important to enter your mind. Deliberately pick the books and magazines you read, films you watch, music and people you listen to, the food you eat and even the drinks you take. I read in an article some time ago that 99% of the things we worry about never happen and so far one of the things that distract us from guarding our mind is worry, once we worry about issues, we remove the guard/ sieve and everything comes in and we lose our foundation. Worry about nothing, plan everything, act timely, focus on God.

    As humans, we are not physical, the only physical thing about us is our body and that is why we need the physical earth bound things like food, body creams, drugs, etc to keep the body. But 90% of our being is spiritual; we are spiritual beings and as spiritual beings we are above the physical/ earthly things. That is why our greatest inspirations are non-physical things like words, music, visions, missions, quests, love, etc. note that even sex is complete in spiritual dimensions and not just at the physical act which is why sex between truly loving married couples of opposite sex is indescribable. Your mind determines how high or low you go in life.

2. Guard your hearts: like I said before, love is strong and non-physical and love is by choice. Love is not blind, what usually happens is that you meet someone whose persona covers all the intricacies your inner man/subconscious is focused on and it is only natural when you look in the mirror you love yourself; if you suddenly see yourself fitting all the descriptions you dreamed of.

Watch your lifestyle: our lifestyle should be our gospel; it should preach the message of who we are, great men act out greatness daily in how they live their life. An example is Jesus Christ of the Bible; He lived a life as guided by the Holy Spirit. But, since the Holy Spirit is spiritual, we can only succeed by toeing the same line if we choose to be like Him.

Every time you see a tree, a tall tree, a huge and massive tree, no matter the height, the roots are usually deeper, the root is the foundation of the tree, and the root feeds and empowers the tree.

What kind of roots do you have and how deep is it? What is the strength and depth of the foundation you are standing on?

No matter who you are, no matter the level you are in your organisation, society or family, you are a leader. This is because leadership is about influence and you don't need a title or position to influence. You have a responsibility to lead from wherever you are, go ahead and lead by increasing your leadership dept and foundation.

Entrepreneurs and business owners have no alternative to leadership, empowered people do it naturally, either by learning or environmental conditioning, and do you want to be empowered? Start leading from where you are today.

EFFICIENT LIFE MANAGEMENT—ELM

Efficient life management (ELM) is organizing, planning and focusing your life in such a way that all the positive expected results manifest at desired levels to you.

ELM is all about you, managing yourself better and achieving more with others. It starts with planning your life, from the end to the present day, from the future to now, from the tombstone to the cradle. It is when you get it right with the main big issues that the small day to day issues will fall into place and have meaning in your life.

ELM teaches you to love yourself. ELM is all about Time management and time is your most precious resource. Your time should always be invested and not spent. Your time is irreplaceable.

Empowered people trade their time for money by creating value.

Everything in life is about value and it revolves around the time you give to it.

ELM is personal and allows you to control how events unfold in your life. It helps you to define the controllable and uncontrollable variables in your life—Uncontrollable variables are those things in our life that we have no control over like where we are born, who we are born to, when the sun rises and when it goes down. The controllable variables are those things in life we can influence, like reading this book, when we sleep, when we eat, going to work, etc. we should concentrate on molding the controllable variables in our lives to fit our life plan and focus on them and allow the uncontrollable variables take their course without worrying about them.

ELM helps you to balance your time and energy for mental, emotional, physical and spiritual activities.

There is no one best method or route to Effective Life Management, it is all about using what works best for you.

It always starts with asking you the question—with all the information I have now and I could live my life all over again, will I live it as before?

It also involves the willingness to make necessary sacrifices to live an empowered life.

The following are tools you can use to guide you in effectively planning your time and life.

Goal maps[xvi]:

This involves 7 questions;

1. What do you want to achieve?
2. Order: which goals take priority?

3. Draw: communicate your goal to your sub consciousness
4. Why; identify your emotional drivers
5. When; define your timeline
6. How; what are the actions you will need to take?
7. Who; choose the people or organisations that can support you.

An illustration is below

A GOAL MAP

Pros and cons:

This is used mainly for deciding between 2 options. This is especially when the 2 options benefit your goal equally. This means, you must have known and clearly defined your goals before you can use this tool.

A typical example will be using a life-balance one where your goals are getting a promotion at work and learning to speak French for your trip to France for holidays.

You just registered for the classes which will hold every Thursday nights for six weeks starting in two weeks time. Also, in your location, this language classes are hard to enroll for as there is usually a long waiting list to get by and you are not usually allowed to miss classes.

On Wednesday night, the night before your first French class, your boss calls you and asks if you will be available for Thursday night as a very senior company executive will be coming round for dinner and your presence will make good on your points for promotion coming soon. All you need do is set up a decision template on a sheet of paper as below;

	Dinner	Class
Pros	- Good for promotion - Good opportunity	- Only six classes - Already registered - Will make holiday fun
cons	- Already committed - Short notice - Should not adversely affect promotion	Will miss the whole course

PROS & CONS TABLE

Looking at the table above, your decision might be to thank your boss for the opportunity but decline the offer as you are already busy for that period and even promise to arrange dinner the next time the executive is in town.

Note that this is usually a method to assist you in clarifying your thoughts and not the decision maker in it because even if you chose to not make a decision at all but just go for the dinner, it is a decision.

It is usually good to set your decision out on a sheet of paper as this will be written down and it helps your thought pattern, but if you have electronic media that can achieve same, please go ahead.

Time style:

Effective life management is a matter of style—working with your strong personality and delegating the rest.

It is based on the principle that there is no right way to manage your time except your way.

1. 'T's are good decision makers and can whip up a task list in no time.
2. 'I's are great enthusiasts and can get any show on the road
3. 'M' has tireless patience and are excellent team players
4. 'E's are meticulous and will always finish the job on time and within budget.

Understand your own time style so you can conduct yourself accordingly; enlist help in areas of personal weaknesses.

This is better illustrated in the next diagram—

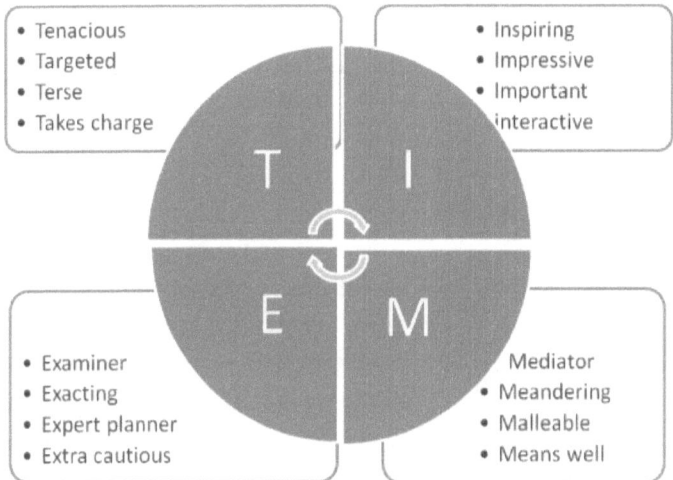

- Tenacious
- Targeted
- Terse
- Takes charge

- Inspiring
- Impressive
- Important
  interactive

- Examiner
- Exacting
- Expert planner
- Extra cautious

Mediator
- Meandering
- Malleable
- Means well

TIME STYLE DIAGRAM.

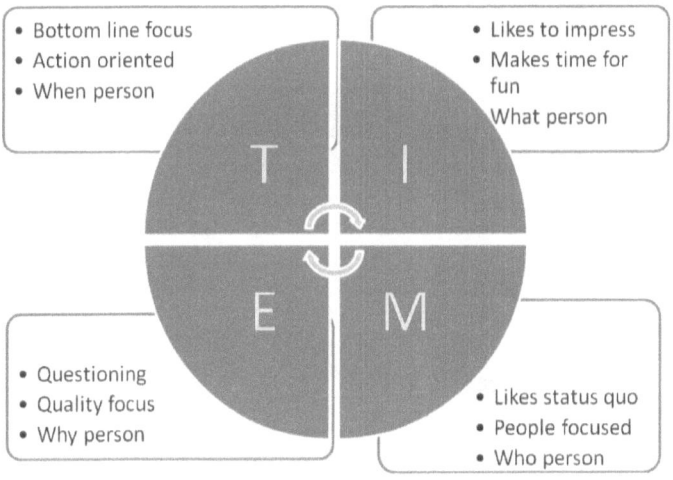

- Bottom line focus
- Action oriented
- When person

- Likes to impress
- Makes time for fun
  What person

- Questioning
- Quality focus
- Why person

- Likes status quo
- People focused
- Who person

TIME STYLE DIAGRAM.

Know your time style and work with it today.

You can get more information on this in Simon Phillips' book—Time Management 24/7: How to double your effectiveness. McGraw-hill Professional, Berkshire, UK, 2002.

PRIORITY QUADRANT

It involves prioritizing your activities and deciding:

1. Which activity directly affects your goal/objective
2. Which activity indirectly affects your goal/objective
3. Which activity does not in any way affect your goal/objective

You focus on, spend more time and energy on activities in 1 and 2 above and completely eliminate activities in 3 above. This is better illustrated below;

TIME QUARDRANT

This is listing all the activities in your life and dividing them into 4 quadrants

This can be better illustrated by the diagram below;

	URGENT	NOT URGENT
IMPORTANT	✓ Crises ✓ Pressing problems ✓ Door bell ringing ✓ Baby crying ✓ Some calls to make ✓ Some projects with deadlines 1	2 ✓ Fitness program ✓ Planning ✓ Relationship building ✓ New opportunities ✓ Recreation ✓ vocation
NOT IMPORTANT	3 ✓ calls to make ✓ distractions ✓ interruptions ✓ some meetings ✓ popular activities ✓ some mails	4 ✓ Gossip ✓ Time wasters ✓ Pleasure activities ✓ Trivia ✓ Some mails

4 QUADRANT TIME MANAGEMENT SYSTEM

It entails putting our lives in perspective and dealing with the issues/activities that are urgent and important (quadrant 1) first then next in line are issues that are not urgent but important (quadrant 2), then issues that are not important but urgent (quadrant 3) before finally attending issues that are not urgent and not important (quadrant 4).

OTHER TOOLS

Other tools you need in this your empowerment journey through ELM are:

- ✓ Use organizers (digital and manual). Stop muddling up activities, organize yourself, and don't jump into events as they come, plan your life and your time. Before committing to any activity, check your organizer to be sure you have time for it.
- ✓ Set daily priority lists/"TO DO lists". Start and end each day with a list of activities to accomplish and those you have accomplished. Your daily, weekly, monthly, annual plans should be in line to your defined primary life goal.
- ✓ Delegation/'other peoples time'. Use the power of team work and the advantage of other people's time to achieve your goals. Delegate as much as possible, it is also a way of training and empowering others around you.
- ✓ Saying 'NO', learn to use the power of the word 'NO'. Say no to time wasters, say no to quadrant 4 activities, and say no to those activities/requests that do not contribute to your goals.
- ✓ Use your diary
- ✓ Use your computers, 'Tablets', I-pods
- ✓ Use your mobile phones, I-phones
- ✓ Use the web

PLANNING

A lot of our discussion so far has been on planning, from goals to self definition to retirement to empowerment.

This word cannot be overemphasized. It is what strategy is all about; we do it every day either consciously or unconsciously.

What we want to do here is just bring it to your conscious mind so you act on it deliberately and thereby achieve more results in your life.

No one goes to war without a strategy and a war strategy is your plan on how you will defeat your opponent in battle. We strategize daily on issues like how to get our promotions, win a customer, how to be in our boss' good books, win the board of directors over, holidays, and so much more. This means we plan every moment of the day.

The plan here now is asking you to put your life in perspective using the tools and guides presented and squeeze out all the juice of incremental positive results in achieving your life mission starting from when you are in paid employment through to the day you die.

Your plans should be flexible enough to be adjusted to meet with the realities of the times. It should cover all your goals and aspirations and should be in writing. Your plans should be easily accessible and available for you to assess daily or at very regular intervals.

Your plans should always ask the questions what? When? Why? Who? How? Your plans should have answers to these questions. It should be able to say what it is you are embarking on, when are you going on this journey and when will each defined milestone be achieved. Why do you want to go on this journey and who will you be taking with you, what will be the role of each person in your team and how are they expected to accomplish their roles. How will you go about starting and concluding this journey, what will it cost you and how do you plan on getting this money and how do you plan on paying back the money.

Your plan can be a one page document or a one thousand page document.

As an employee, you plan your exit from your first day at work; you also start implementing your plan from your first day at work.

Your plans should always be defined, have a body, state benefits, pros and cons and have conclusions.

Your plans should be able to ignite and drive your passion; it should also be able to open your eyes to the vision.

Your plan should be transferrable and should be able to leave a legacy on completion.

OTHER PEOPLES TIME

Learn to use other peoples time positively. Use the power of team work. Delegate! Delegate! Delegate!

Draw up your plans and goals, share it with others and enroll them into your life mission.

[A plan to live a life of empowerment is a life to empower others.]

If you can draw up a plan that ignites your passion, your passion will light up others and you will soon be a burning forest.

As an employee, always take on as much work as comes your way and as you climb up the ladder, delegate everything (at least almost) but lead from your heart.

A plan to live a life of empowerment is a life to empower others. To achieve this, you must have a life purpose and a life plan, vision and mission that are bigger than even a thousand of you if possible. This makes it mandatory to recruit a team of leaders (not followers) to come along with you on your success journey.

If you have a dream that does not includes others positively then it is not a dream, just a commercial break.

History has it in loads; the only people that have succeeded in life to outlive their persons are those whose dreams were greater than them; Dr. Martin Luther King Jnr[xvii], Nelson Mandela[xviii], Mahatma Gandhi[xix], Jesus Christ[xx], Abraham Lincoln[xxi], and so much more. They achieved so much and are still talked about and influencing people today because they had very big dreams and recruited others to join them in achieving their dreams. They empowered not just themselves but others and made use of the power of other people's time.

To use this principle effectively, you must be passionate about your dream, you must have a clearly laid out plan (it does not need to be specific), and you must be able to show others what is in it for them, learn to love; show, appreciate and share love. Have true and genuine respect for their time and ensure that the roles they are given will empower them positively. Learn the art and science of public speaking and look for every opportunity to share and recruit your team daily.

Create value in all your plans and all the people and resources you need will naturally flow to you.

Note that all we have listed above are not all applicable by you and there are so many more ways to empowerment. I don't expect you to use all of them but use the ones or combinations of techniques that best suits you at every point in time in your empowerment journey.

Also, it is not a story of overnight success; it is a story of continual learning, adjustments, victories, losses but progress.

Give value to your life, empower yourself mentally, physically and spiritually. Mental empowerment is applying the techniques and methods that best suits you as stated in this book. Physical empowerment involves living a physically fit healthy life style while spiritual empowerment is empowering yourself in the supernatural. The supernatural is primary to your empowerment as anything that happens in the physical must always happen first in the supernatural. Hold on strong to your faith, if it seems not to be working for you, try a better one. For me, the one and only faith that has worked is faith in Jesus Christ.

CHAPTER 5

BE DELIBERATE IN YOUR ACTS

Invest in other peoples' lives. For example, be of assistance to any victim of retrenchment. It is a golden opportunity to positively impact someone's life! Invest in paying school fees for someone that cannot afford it, join an NGO, and contribute positively to your community, look for how to add value to your colleagues be they your line mates, superiors or subordinates.

That day will come when you will have to leave your paid employment either voluntarily or otherwise, the earlier you start to prepare for life after employment the better for you.

Saving or investing for retirement or post-work is good, but you require more than money to sustain yourself post-work. You need a vocation or daily activity.

You must consciously fight the spirit of procrastination.

While implementing your plan, never forget that you are presently an employee.

Therefore, do not let your personal business encroach on your employer's time for any reason. When you get to that point where your time is torn tightly between the two ends, it's time to face your business.

You cannot serve two masters. Follow your heart. If your mind and heart is now all about your business, follow that path. Do not try to juggle it too much, else at one point, all the cookies will crumble and you will lose at both ends.

Work the way you would want your workers to work for you.

A bad employee today never gets good staff tomorrow.

Do not engage in activities that will kill your employers business.

As you work and plan and implement, ask God for wisdom to do it right.

If and when you get to the point where you are transiting from an employee to being an employer ensure you set up a transition plan for yourself to ensure a smooth exit. Keep it as short and quick as possible.

If it is possible, discuss your proposed exit with your present employer.

When you get to the point of exit, ensure you have a contingency plan too if your current business plan does not work as planned.

You can only succeed.

CHAPTER 6

THE FUTURE

We know where we are coming from; we know where we are, so where are we going to? Is there a future for paid employment especially in Nigeria?

Yes, there is a future and a great one indeed.

Please note that I am not asking you to leave your fat paying jobs today, what I am saying is that you should get a life and decide what part of the divide you want to be; do you want to be a slave tied to your salary or do you want to be free working because you want to and you enjoy it and leave when the need arises and not when you are thrown out to nothingness.

Presently, as an employee, no matter how much you earn, you are not in the upper class, and your highest level is the upper middle class. But I want you in the upper class.

Also, it is not everyone that is cut out to be an entrepreneur, some of us are intrapreneurs[xxii], and we do well and excel and achieve our life mission as employees. Such people fail woefully if they are put out there in the jungle of entrepreneurship and investment.

An Intrapreneur is a person with Entrepreneur skills and abilities who is able to deploy such skills excellently as an employee in his/her employer's organisation but will fail woefully if allowed/released to demonstrate same skills when running their business independently.

If you fall in this category, don't move an inch out of paid employment, stay there and run it as if it were your own.

For you who are cut out to remain in paid employment, I need us to know some facts;

Basically, a business system is divided into three namely the marketing department, the operations department and the support units.

Starting with operations, more emphasis will be on automation and outsourcing. The bank teller for example already has the ATM machine to contend with, thanks to this machine, we can bank 24/7; we don't need to carry much cash around and customers do not need to meet those boring faces in the banking hall to make withdrawals or stand in those long queues. But, this machine has helped reduce the queues in the banking halls, it has also helped reduce the number of tellers needed in a banking hall and over time, this same machine will help to further reduce the number of tellers in a banking hall to a minimum.

Banks can also consider outsourcing their customer service function and account opening will now be handled by the account officers as approved by the heads of operations. This would drastically reduce staff costs and impact directly on revenue.

Bank marketing will no longer be based on cheque collection and sentiments like it happens in Nigeria presently. It will basically be a business relationship; a system that would encourage specialization and gathering of expertise in various sectors of the economy and finance for which clients will be encouraged to do business with you. Less cheque collectors will be needed and more specialists/consultants will be needed. Therefore, the less expertise you have in your employment, the fewer customers you will have, and the less expertise you as a bank staff have, the less your services will be required in banking. Only empowered staff will remain.

The bank would require more of the support unit to run and administer its various outsourced services and its vast infrastructure. But the support unit too will give rise to proliferation of specialized bank support services for which reason competition will get high along with professionalism and banking as a whole will be better for it.

This means that for you to stay and survive in the employee jungle you have to sharpen your skills, specialize and upgrade else you will only go extinct and become a museum piece. Get empowered!

If you fall into the divide of employee for life, ensure you invest your money. Never spend all of it. You can do without those loans for financing your luxurious lifestyle. Let your investments buy you a luxurious lifestyle.

To achieve this, set up a life investment plan; ensure that at least 50% of your annual income goes into this for at least 60 to 120 months. These investments includes forming and running investment clubs, joining co-operatives, venture capital, stock markets, real estate and so much more.

Set up an investment portfolio, when you get too busy to manage it hand it over to a trust company to run with you and not for you.

Sit with your lawyer and draw up your will.

An important note here is that you should ensure you engage in one venture at a time. Allow that one grow to a sustainable level before moving to the next one. It is not advisable to engage two or three at once. There is great power in focus.

You can partner with us at the **COINBOX ENTREPRENEUR NETWORK.** If interested go to www.coinboxng.com.

Dear employee, I close with what I said at the beginning of this book—*give yourself a life, a life of empowerment.*

ENDNOTES

i   http://www.investopedia.com/articles/economics/09/lehman-brothers-collapse.asp#axzz2BjuWZKCq
http://en.wikipedia.org/wiki/Lehman_Brothers

ii   Proverbs chapter 13 verse 22 (new king James version of the BIBLE)

iii   NGO stands for Non-governmental organisation. These are usually private not-for-profit organisations set up to raise funds to support causes of various kinds like the better life for rural women program in Nigeria.

iv   The Maxwell leadership Bible, 2002, by Maxwell Motivation, Inc. John C. Maxwell, Executive Editor. Thomas Nelson Bibles.

v   THE 8TH HABIT from effectiveness to greatness by Stephen R. Covey. Simon and Schuster UK Ltd, 2004.

vi   http://www.slideshare.net/ChamnanNop/stephen-covey-the-9010-principle

vii   Genesis chapter 2 verse 18-New King James Version. Thomas Nelson Bibles, a division of Thomas Nelson, Inc. Maxwell Leadership Bible, 2002 by Maxwell Motivation, Inc.

viii   FAILING FORWARD Turning mistakes into stepping stones for success by John C. Maxwell. Thomas Nelson Publishers, 2000.

ix   http://en.wikipedia.org/wiki/Mentorship

x   http://en.wikipedia.org/wiki/Empowerment

xi   Time Management 24/7: How to double your effectiveness by Simon Phillips. McGraw-hill Professional, Berkshire, UK, 2002.

xii   Time Management 24/7: How to double your effectiveness by Simon Phillips. McGraw-hill Professional, Berkshire, UK, 2002.

xiii   The book of Luke Chapter 6, Verse 45, New King James version, Maxwell Leadership Bible, Maxwell Motivation, Inc. 2002.

xiv   https://www.bible.com/bible/114/mat.7.msg

xv   Maxwell Leadership Bible, 2002, by Maxwell Motivation, Inc.

xvi   https://www.goalmappingonline.com/

xvii   http://farm1.static.flickr.com/183/410995180_3562af2ad6.jpg

xviii Time Management 24/7: How to double your effectiveness by Simon Phillips. McGraw-hill Professional, Berkshire, UK, 2002.

xix   http://www.salmanahsan.com/4-quadrants-time-management-system/

xx   http://www.change-management-coach.com/stephen-covey.html

xxi   http://en.wikipedia.org/wiki/Martin_Luther_King,_Jr.

xxii   http://www.nelsonmandela.org/content/page/biography

xxiii http://www.biography.com/people/
mahatma-gandhi-9305898

xxiv http://christianity.about.com/od/newtestamentpeople/p/
jesuschrist.htm

xxv http://www.whitehouse.gov/about/presidents/
abrahamlincoln

xxvi http://www.intrapreneur.com/MainPages/History/
Dictionary.html: in-tra-pre-neur (In¹tre-pre-nur) n. A
person within a large corporation who takes direct
responsibility for turning an idea into a profitable finished
product through assertive risk-taking and innovation
[intra(corporate) + (ENTRE)PRENEUR.] -inftrapre-nouri-al
adj. -intra-pre-neuri-al-ism n. -in'trapre-neuri-al-ly adv.

REFERENCES

1. Ayo Emakhiomhe. LIFE AFTER BANKING: Attaining financial freedom during and after paid employment. Coinbox Limited, Lagos, Nigeria. 2012.

2. Simon Phillips. TIME MANAGEMENT 24/7: How to double your effectiveness. Mcgrawhill Professional, Shoppenhangers Road, Berkshire. 2002.

3. Stephen R. Covey.THE 8TH HABIT, FROM EFFECTIVENESS TO GREATNESS. FranklinCovey Co. 2004.

4. John C. Maxwell. MAXWELL LEADERSHIP BIBLE. New KING JAMES version. Thomas Nelson Bibles, Thomas Nelson, Inc. 2002.

ABOUT THE AUTHOR

The author is a business development consultant. He consults for SME's and start ups or businesses that want to move to the next level and cannot seem to find that next step.

He has succeeded in helping a lot of companies and individuals start off, find their feet and raise funds for their business.

He has over 10 years of banking experience spanning several positions from FCMB to Zenith bank, Guarantee Trust bank, Oceanic Bank and Ecobank all in Nigeria where he bowed out as the manager of one of their branches in Apapa, Lagos.

He has his B.SC (HONS) in Accounting from Olabisi Onabanjo University, Ogun state, Nigeria, an MBA from

Obafemi Awolowo University, Ile-Ife, Nigeria. He is an associate of the Nigerian Institute of Management (NIM), a member of the Institute of chartered Economists of Nigeria (ICEN), a member of the Institute of Operations research (IOR) in the United Kingdom, a member of the leadership system of Daystar Christian Center, Lagos.

He is the co-founder and vice president of the Coinbox Entrepreneur Network and MD/CEO of COINBOX LIMITED (a business support company).

He is a real estate developer and he is also the co-founder of Coinbox Cooperative multipurpose society, a Cooperative that supports small businesses.

He is married to the love of his life and better half—Frances with two angels for kids.

He can be reached by email at emakhiomheayo@yahoo.com

You can go to www.coinboxlimited.blogspot.com for other entrepreneurial/investment resources and www.zerofactorleadership.blogspot.com for self development and leadership resources. https://www.facebook.com/pages/AYO-Emakhiomhe/509162689124196 https://twitter.com/ayoemakhiomhe